Disney Princess Celebrations

Disney PRINCESS

CELEBRATE with Belle

Plan a *Beauty and the Beast* Party

Niki Ahrens

Lerner Publications ◆ Minneapolis

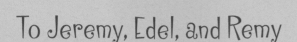

To Jeremy, Edel, and Remy

Lerner Publications Company
An imprint of Lerner Publishing Group, Inc.
241 First Avenue North
Minneapolis, MN 55401 USA

For reading levels and more information, look up this title at www.lernerbooks.com.

Main body text set in Billy Infant.
Typeface provided by Sparky Type.

Library of Congress Cataloging-in-Publication Data

Names: Ahrens, Niki, 1979- author.
Title: Celebrate with Belle : plan a Beauty and the beast party / Niki Ahrens.
Description: Minneapolis : Lerner Publications , [2020] | Series: Disney princess celebrations | Includes bibliographical references and index. | Audience: Ages 6–10. | Audience: Grades K–3.
Identifiers: LCCN 2019016703 (print) | LCCN 2019980951 (ebook) | ISBN 9781541572768 (library binding : alk. paper) | ISBN 9781541587199 (paperback : alk. paper)
Subjects: LCSH: Beauty and the beast (Motion picture : 1991)—Juvenile literature. | Beauty and the beast (Motion picture : 1991) | Party decorations—Juvenile literature. | Children's parties—Juvenile literature.
Classification: LCC TT900.P3 A433 2020 (print) | LCC TT900.P3 (ebook) | DDC 745.594/1—dc23

LC record available at https://lccn.loc.gov/2019016703
LC ebook record available at https://lccn.loc.gov/2019980951

Manufactured in the United States of America
1-46543-47588-7/3/2019

Table of Contents

An Adventurous Celebration 4

Wise Hosting Tips 6

Book Invitations 8

Lumiere Decorations 12

Teacup Cocoa Pops 16

Maurice's Maker Space 18

Would You Pass Me the Tea, Please? . . 20

Bookmark Party Favors 22

Enchanting Thank-You Roses 24

Imagine Your Adventure! 28

Glossary 30

To Learn More 31

Index 32

An Adventurous Celebration

Do you like to go on adventures? Belle dreamed of traveling beyond her village. Plan a magical party celebrating courage and new experiences! You'll need to do these things:

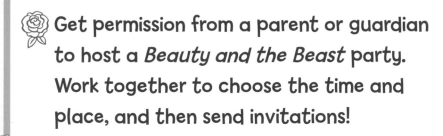

- Get permission from a parent or guardian to host a *Beauty and the Beast* party. Work together to choose the time and place, and then send invitations!

- Make your decorations, party favors, and treats.

- Show leadership skills by guiding guests through party activities.

- Afterward, clean up and send thank-you notes to your guests.

Wise Hosting Tips

🌹 Make sure to be well rested before your exciting adventure.

🌹 Be aware of your guests' food allergies.

🌹 Protect your craft workspace by covering it with newspaper.

🌹 Be responsible by washing your hands before making treats.

🌹 Wholeheartedly welcome every guest to join the celebration.

🌹 Recycle many of your materials after the fun!

Book Invitations

The pages of Belle's favorite books take her on exciting adventures. Invite your friends to be your guests with book invitations.

Be My Guest

Be My Guest

Materials

- cardstock

- scissors

- markers

- ruler

- glue stick

- 12-inch (30 cm) piece of ribbon

1. Fold a cardstock sheet in half. Trim off the corners on the top right and bottom left.

2. At the top left corner, draw a short diagonal line.

3. Use a ruler to draw a straight line across the book from the end of the short line to the top trimmed corner. Draw another straight line from the bottom trimmed corner to the end of the short line.

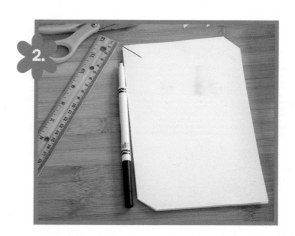

4. Decorate your book cover.

5. Glue a ribbon inside the fold.

6. Write your invitation inside, including the party date, time, and place. Send one to each guest!

6.

Be My Guest

You are invited to be my guest!

Date:

Time:

Place:

Please bring a book to donate! ♡

Party Tip! Be Earth-Friendly
Invite your guests to bring a gently used book for a book drive. After the party, donate the collected books to a charity or library.

Lumiere Decorations

Lumiere helps Belle while she stays in Beast's castle. Brighten up your party with Lumiere candelabra decorations.

Materials

- 2 clothespins

- drinking straw

- pencil

- 4 mini muffin liners

- pipe cleaner

- craft glue

- 2 cotton balls

- 4-inch (10 cm) cardstock square

- double-sided tape

1. Clip two clothespins to the end of a straw to stand it upright.

2. Use a pencil to poke a hole through the center of a muffin liner. Slide the muffin liner, cup down, down the straw.

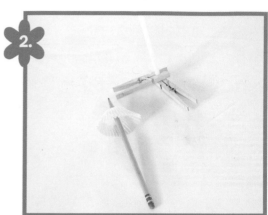

3. Wrap a pipe cleaner's center around the straw's center two times. Bend elbows into the pipe cleaner arms.

4. Slide a muffin liner, cup up, onto each arm. Fold the pipe cleaner tips down.

5. Glue a cotton ball to the inside of each of the second and third muffin liners.

6. Poke a hole with a pencil in the fourth muffin liner's center. Slide this onto the straw.

7. Draw Lumiere's face on the cardstock. Roll this and tape it to make a candlestick.

8. Add this candlestick to the straw.

Teacup Cocoa Pops

Teacup Chip helps welcome Belle to an elegant dinner. Serve fancy marshmallow cocoa pops inspired by Chip.

Materials

- lollipop sticks

- 12-inch (30 cm) pieces of ribbon (optional)

- small cups

Ingredients

- jumbo marshmallows

- frosting

- sprinkles

- mini chocolate chips

- mini pretzels

1. Carefully place a marshmallow on a lollipop stick.

2. Spread a thin layer of frosting on the top half of the marshmallow.

3. Dip the frosted marshmallow in sprinkles and mini chocolate chips.

4. Break a C-shape off a pretzel. Dip the ends of the pretzel piece in frosting. Attach the C-shape to the marshmallow to make a teacup handle.

5. If you are using a ribbon, tie it around the lollipop stick under the marshmallow.

6. Make enough teacup pops for your celebration. Set the teacup pops in small cups to serve to guests.

Maurice's Maker Space

Belle's father uses tools and materials to invent machines. Have a party station where guests can play and create art.

Materials

- trays

- glue sticks

- craft glue

- patterned tape

- clear tape

- scissors

- craft supplies such as felt squares, cardstock, cardboard tubes, egg cartons, toothpicks, bottle caps, and craft sticks

1. Place trays of crafty materials out for your guests to use.

2. Have fun using supplies and your imagination to make neat crafts and art.

3. Share your ideas and creations!

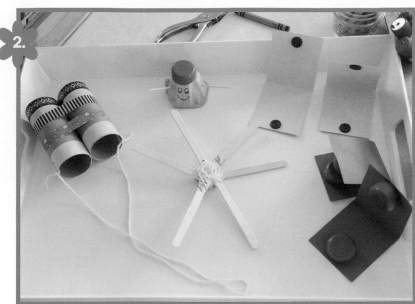

Party Tip! Be Respectful

It's okay for your guests to use maker space supplies in different ways. Some might just want to tinker, and some might make or invent a craft. If everyone has fun, that's success!

Would You Pass Me the Tea, Please?

Mrs. Potts and Chip serve tea. Have fun passing around tea packets and acting out *Beauty and the Beast* characters.

Materials

- unopened dry tea packets

- fun music

- music player

- helper to play and pause music

1. Invite guests to sit in small circles of three or four. Larger circles work well too!

2. Give each small circle an unopened packet of dry tea.

3. Start the music and ask guests to pass the tea packets to the friend sitting on their left.

4. Keep passing the tea packets while the music plays.

5. When the music stops, players pause. The players holding the tea act as a character from *Beauty and the Beast*. The other players in the circle try to guess the character.

6. Invite every guest to take a turn acting before ending the game.

Bookmark Party Favors

Belle doesn't like to set a good book down. Send recycled bookmarks home with your guests for their own reading adventures.

Materials

- scissors

- empty tissue box

- ruler

- hole punch

- 12-inch (30 cm) piece of ribbon

- stickers

- markers

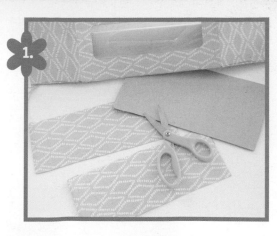

1. Cut a tissue box's sides apart at the folds to make cardboard sheets.

2. From the edge of a cardboard sheet, trace around half of a ruler. Cut this shape out.

3. Punch a hole at the top of the bookmark.

4. Fold a ribbon piece in half. Thread the fold through the hole to make a loop. Pull the ribbon's ends through the loop. Keep pulling until the loop is tied tight.

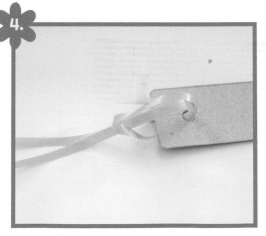

5. Decorate the bookmark with stickers and markers. Make one for each guest!

Party Tip! Did You Know?

Bookmarks have been used by readers for more than a thousand years. The earliest bookmarks were often made from leather or ivory. Paper and other materials became more commonly used after 1880.

Enchanting Thank-You Roses

The Beast's magic rose was a reminder for him to learn to love. Thank your party guests with an enchanting rose.

Materials

- metallic marker
- red paper half sheets
- black pen or marker

1. Use a metallic marker to draw an oval near the top of the paper.

2. Draw a small spiral in the oval.

3. Draw a heart around the oval.

Party Tip! Did You Know?

Besides growing roses for their beauty, people throughout history have used them for medicine, tea, and perfume.

4. Then draw the bottom of a heart underneath the first heart. Add small leaves under this.

5. Give your rose a stem with leaves.

6. On the back, use a black marker or pen to write a thank-you message.

7. Send an enchanting rose to each guest!

Belle looked for adventure in the pages of books. Her knowledge, courage, and kindness helped her when she embarked on a real adventure.

Let Belle's curiosity and confidence inspire you as you plan your celebration. Dream up ideas and invent a party that is thrilling for you and your guests.

Glossary

candelabra: a candleholder for more than one candle

elegant: quality and stylish

embark: to start something new, often a journey or other adventure

enchanting: especially charming or magical

guest: someone who attends an event or party

host: to hold an event or party for guests

ivory: a material that comes from the tusks of animals

metallic: shiny and metallike in appearance

To Learn More

BOOKS

Disney Storybook Artists. *Learn to Draw Disney's Classic Fairy Tales: Featuring Cinderella, Snow White, Belle, and All Your Favorite Fairy Tale Characters!* Lake Forest, CA: Walter Foster Jr., 2018.
Learn to draw your favorite characters from Disney fairy tales.

Kington, Emily. *Rad Recycled Art*. Minneapolis: Hungry Tomato, 2019.
Recycle trash into art treasures.

WEBSITES

Belle's Crown Crafting Project
https://family.disney.com/craft/belles-crown/
Create your very own royal crown just like Belle's.

"12 Things in *Beauty and the Beast* That Are More Peculiar Than Belle"
https://ohmy.disney.com/movies/2015/05/09/12-things-in
-beauty-and-the-beast-that-are-more-peculiar-than-belle/
Enjoy interesting and odd moments that happened in Belle's world.

Index

adventures, 4, 6, 8, 22, 29
art, 18-19

books, 10-11, 22, 29

candelabra, 12

decorations, 4, 12

friends, 8, 21

guests, 4, 6, 8, 11, 17-19, 21-24, 27, 29

music, 20-21

play, 18, 21

roses, 24, 26-27

tea, 20-21
treats, 4, 6

PHOTO CREDITS

Additional photos: art_of_sun/Shutterstock.com, p. 2; Julia Sudnitskaya/Shutterstock.com, p. 3; Rawpixel.com/Shutterstock.com, p. 5B; KlavdiyaV/Shutterstock.com, p. 5T; Kostikova Natalia/Shutterstock.com, p. 7T; gosphotodesign/Shutterstock.com, p. 7B. Cover and design elements: Susii/Shutterstock.com (balloons); YamabikaY/Shutterstock.com (glitter); surachet khamsuk/Shutterstock.com (glitter).